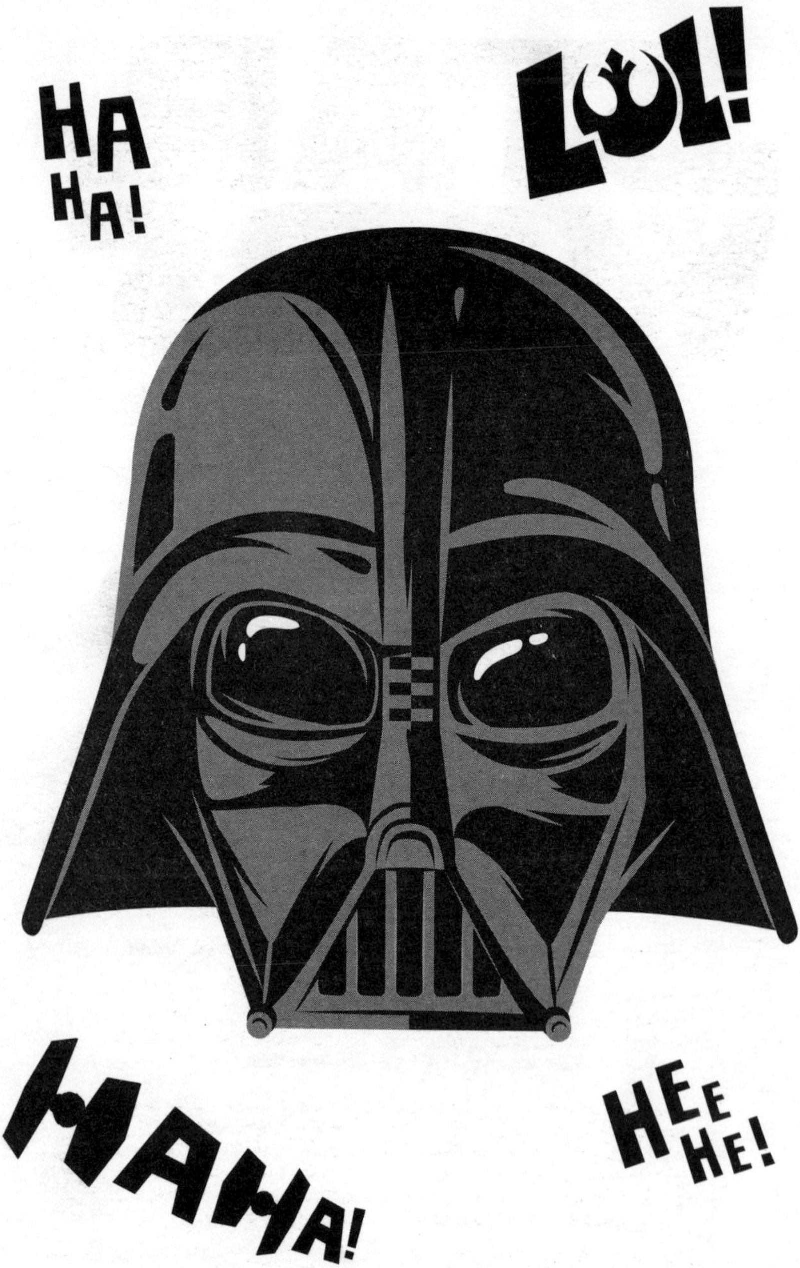

HA HA!
LOL!
HAHA!
HEE HE!

Joke Book

EGMONT
We bring stories to life

First published in Great Britain 2015 by Egmont UK Limited
The Yellow Building, 1 Nicholas Road, London W11 4AN
© & ™ 2015 Lucasfilm Ltd.

Written by Emil Fortune
Designed by Richie Hull, Joe Bolder
Illustrated by Gregory Sokol

ISBN 978 1 4052 7630 6
59570/7
Printed in Great Britain

Find more great *Star Wars* books at www.egmont.co.uk/starwars

Stay safe online. Any website addresses listed in this book are
correct at the time of going to print. However, Egmont is not
responsible for content hosted by third parties. Please be aware
that online content can be subject to change and websites can
contain content that is unsuitable for children. We advise that all
children are supervised when using the internet.

AT THE PALACE OF
JABBA
THE HUTT

Jester! I'm bored. I command you to tell me a joke – and make it funny, or I'll feed you to the rancor.

Yes, master!

A man lives next door to the Jedi Temple, and he keeps hearing a mysterious noise coming from it. He can't work out what it is. Not knowing is driving him crazy. One day he decides he can't take it any more – he just has to know where it's coming from, so he goes in to ask.

"Can I help you?" asks a Jedi Master.

"I just want to know what that noise is," says the man.

"I'm sorry, I can't tell you," says the Master, "as you're not a Jedi."

"How do I become a Jedi, then?" says the man. "I must know!"

"You must think about the Force, silently and alone, for five years," says the Master. "Then return to me." So the man goes away and thinks for five years, completely alone.

"Excellent," says the Master, when he returns.

"Now: please can I find out what that noise is?" asks the man.

"I'm sorry, you are not a Jedi!" says the Master. "Now you must spend five years in the deserts of Tatooine, eating nothing but sand, drinking nothing but ... sand juice, I guess – then return, and we shall see."

The man goes into the desert and lives there in a hole in the sand for the next five years. He's covered in sand the whole time.

He's sick of the sight of sand. Don't even get him started about the Jawas. When his time is up, he returns to the Temple.

"Well done," says the Jedi Master.

"Can I find out what that—" says the man.

"I'm sorry, you are not a Jedi! But here is your final test: as a test of your faith in the Force, you must fling yourself off the tallest tower in the city."

The man isn't really sure about this, but it's been ten years, and he is desperate to find out what the mysterious noise is. So he climbs to the top of the tallest tower in the city and flings himself off. Just before he hits the ground, he stops in mid-air – it's the Jedi Master, holding him up with the power of the Force.

"Well done! You are now a Jedi," says the Master. "Come with me to the Temple, and there you will find the answers you seek!"

They walk in to the Temple, give the secret Jedi password to the guards, and are let in to a special room where the Master unlocks a heavy iron gate with three locks. Behind it is a long dark tunnel. At the end of the tunnel is a ladder leading down in to a deep dark cavern.

They climb down. The Master lights a candle and they make their way through the cave, picking their way over the rocks, until they come to a vast stone door. From behind the door the man can hear the mysterious sound, echoing out of the darkness.

The Master rolls the door aside, and behind it is a small room with a brass chest. The noise is coming from inside the box.

The man steps forward, grasps the handle, and opens the chest to reveal...

... well, I'd tell you, but you're not a Jedi.

In loving memory

R.I.P.

So that's what happened to Jabba's last jester! We were all really sad to see him get eaten by the rancor, especially me, because he owed me a thousand credits.

Good evening, everyone, I'm your host for this evening, Salacious Crumb. Welcome to Jabba's palace!

We have many famous faces here tonight, all competing to see who is the funniest stand-up comedian in the galaxy. And YOU, the audience, get to decide! Just write your score for each contestant in the space provided. We'll see who wins at the end, and who's a rancor snack!

Darth Vader's armour is very impressive. It must have cost an arm and a leg.

n_n

HEE HEE!

Seriously, folks, his whole left side got cut off. But I hear he's all right now.

Impressive

He's had to stop playing cards since he got the robot arm, though. He just can't DEAL with it.

Score:

/10

How can you tell if there's a rancor living in your refrigerator? Claw-prints in the butter.

What did the rancor say when it ate the Wookiee? Mmm ... chewy!

The rancor didn't enjoy eating Jabba's last jester. Apparently he tasted funny.

Bas kah!

Meh.

Score:

/10

Why does Darth Vader wear a black cape? Hmm? Because in the wash, his pink one is.

u_u

Argued with the referee at a rugby match, I did. Try? There was no try.

FUNNY THIS IS!

Emperor Palpatine and Count Dooku have launched their own brands of aftershave. Begun, the Cologne Wars have.

Cologne

A young Padawan joins the Jedi Order. To prove his discipline, a vow of silence he takes. Two words, and two words only, he is allowed to speak, once every seven years.

After seven years, the Jedi council summons him. His two words, they ask for.

"Very draughty," he says. They nod and send him away. Seven more years pass, and back, for his next two words, he comes.

"Bad food," he says. Again, they nod. Seven more years pass, and it is time again for his two words.

"I quit," he says.

"Surprised, I am not," the Grand Master says. "You have done nothing but complain since you got here."

BE-BOP TAWEEEP!

Score:

/10

Dr Evazan has been sentenced to death in twelve star systems, but only a couple of those were for his stand-up act.

Dr Evazan

Admiral Ackbar was held for ransom a while back – it turned out to be the work of squidnappers. Anyway, he's off the hook now, so please, give him a warm welcome.

Admiral Ackbar

Here's Bib Fortuna, Jabba's flunky. It also happens to be the name for what Jabba wears when he's eating fish.

Bib Fortuna

Luke Skywalker is good at two things: moisture farming, and bullseyeing womp rats in his X-34 landspeeder. Naturally he's the Galaxy's last hope.

Luke Skywalker

The Emperor zapped me with lightning bolts. Shocking behaviour!

LOL!

Are there any Sand People in the audience? I'm picking something up on my Tusken Radar.

Yoda hasn't been taking on any new students. He says he's swamped at work.

Mudhole? SLIMY? My home this is!

Three stormtroopers are lost in the Tatooine desert, dying of thirst.

Finally they come to a mysterious slide in the middle of the desert that has instructions at the top: "Slide down and yell the drink of your choice and at the bottom you will find a pool of that beverage."

The three troopers are very excited. The first one slides down yelling "Water!" Splash! He falls into a pool of cool, clear water.

The second trooper slides down yelling "Lemonade!" Splash! He falls into a pool full of it.

The final trooper jumps on the slide, but he's a bit overexcited. "Wheeee!"

HAHA!

Score:

/10

Two stormtroopers crash on Hoth and spot a huge wampa running towards them, so they start sprinting in the other direction.

One yells to the other, "You really think we can outrun that wampa?"

The other one says, "I don't have to ... I just have to outrun you!"

A stormtrooper walks into a doctor's office with a jogan fruit stuck in one ear, a nerf steak stuck in the other, and a grape up his nose.

"I don't feel well, doctor," he says.

"I can see the problem," says the doctor. "You're not eating properly."

Two stormtroopers are searching Tatooine for some missing droids, and have run out of water. They climb a sand dune and spot a row of three tents on the other side.

There's a shopkeeper in the first tent, so they ask for water. "Sorry, no," he says, "all I have is sponge cake." That's not going to help, think the stormtroopers, so they try the second tent.

The shopkeeper in the second tent doesn't have any water either. "Sorry," he says, "all I've got is jelly and whipped cream." They can't drink that, so they head off to the third tent.

o_O

"Do you have any water?" they ask in the the third tent. "No," says the shopkeeper, "just these little multicoloured sprinkles."

The stormtroopers set off to find water, and one says to the other, "That was weird."

"Yes," says the other, "it was a trifle bazaar."

Score:

/10

Heh!

People say I suffer from insanity. That's nonsense. I enjoy every minute of it! Heh, heh, heh!

Why did the Ewok fall out of the tree? It was dead.

Whenever the Death Star blows a planet up, the newspaper runs an orbituary.

Omu`sata!

Score:

/10

Lobot's computerised brain helps keep Cloud City running smoothly. He's a man of few words, so let's hope they're actually funny.

Lobot

YOUR HOST:
SALACIOUS
CRUMB

Dengar is a famous bounty hunter, but he has yet to track down whoever it was that sold him that outfit.

Dengar

What did the wampa say to the tauntaun? "Well, it's been nice gnawing you."

Bah–haha!

Did you hear about the queues at the Jawa hospital? You have to be a little patient.

XD

What do you call a spaceship with a broken air conditioner? A frying saucer.

HA!

Score:

/10

She's the young Senator from Alderaan, plus she's a rebel leader, a crack shot AND she's a Princess. Wow! But is she funny? Let's find out.

Princess Leia

Why did Luke join the gym? He thought the new droids would work out.

L⊙L!

Why did the Wookiee cross the road? It was the chicken's day off.

PAH!

I hear Jabba's on a seafood diet. He sees food, he eats it.

HA!

Score:

/10

I'm sure you've heard of Figrin D'an and his band the Modal Nodes? They're quite famous though he doesn't like to blow his own trumpet (it's more of a clarinet-type-thing.)

Figrin D'an

YOUR HOST:
SALACIOUS CRUMB

4-LOM looks like a bug-eyed monster, but he's actually a droid bounty hunter. (No offence to any of you bug-eyed monsters in the audience.)

4-LOM

I'm giving away my old batteries, if anyone wants them – free of charge.

LOL!

I think I need to go back to droid school for a bit. I'm getting a bit rusty.

As you wish

As a droid, I don't have any brothers – just transistors.

Meh.

Score:

/10

YOUR HOST:
SALACIOUS CRUMB

Mon Mothma doesn't seem like she'd be a natural comedian. "Many Bothans died to bring you these jokes," she told me. What does that even mean?

Mon Mothma

How does Han Solo make a shelter on Hoth? Igloos it together.

HEE HEE!

What's dark, scary, and has three wheels? Darth Vader on a tricycle.

~o

Grrr

Why did the spy stay in bed? He was working undercover.

Score:

/10

HA!

YOUR HOST:
SALACIOUS
CRUMB

Admiral Ozzel wasn't supposed to be here. Darth Vader told him he was going to be in a 'choke book' and I think he misheard him.

Admiral Ozzel

Why does Darth Vader burn his toast? He likes it on the dark side!

LOL!

Hehe

Rebel traitors have hijacked an Imperial soap delivery. Despite our best efforts, they made a clean getaway.

Imperial scientists have invented a way to walk through walls. It's called a 'door'.

Score:

/10

The captain of a pirate ship is under attack by an Imperial ship. He tells his first officer to bring him his red shirt.

His first officer asks him "Why do you want your red shirt?"

The captain replies, "Never let your enemy see you bleed! If I get hit, nobody will be able to tell."

The next day the first officer rushes on to the bridge. "Captain! Two hundred Imperial ships coming our way!"

The captain sighs and says, "Bring me my brown trousers!"

I don't like you!

Did you hear about the violent Power Droid? It was arrested for assault and battery.

HA HA!

Score:

/10

Boba Fett is the galaxy's scariest bounty hunter – please give him a warm welcome. No disintegrations, Boba!

Boba Fett

Keep track with this handy scorecard!

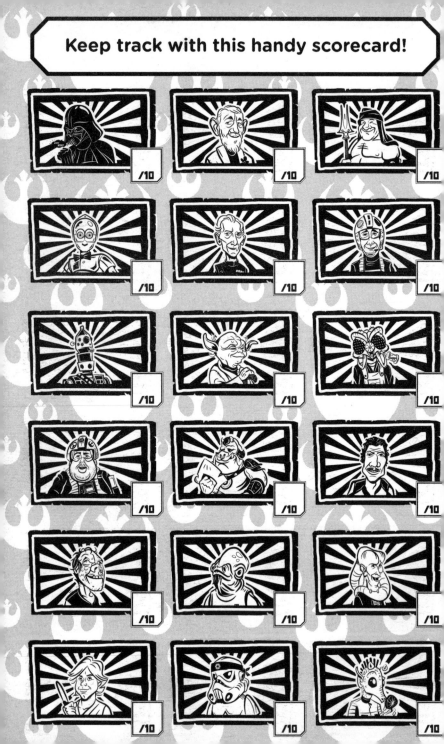

Ladies, gentlemen, droids, cyborgs and Force spirits: I added up all the scores and am pleased to announce that the winner of tonight's comedy contest is the great and powerful Jabba the Hutt!

He also won the raffle, the beauty contest, the long jump, musical chairs, pass-the-parcel, the rancor egg hunt, and pin-the-tail-on-the-tauntaun.

(Sometimes I wonder if he cheats?)

Thanks for coming, and remember: laugh it up, fuzzballs!